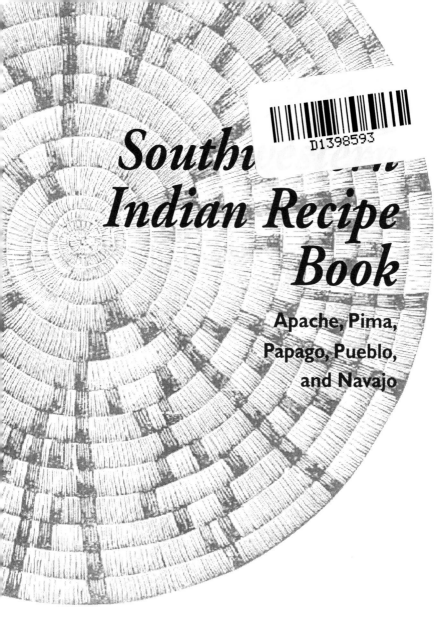

Southwestern Indian Recipe Book

Apache, Pima, Papago, Pueblo, and Navajo

Traditional aboriginal recipes—
with a few modern variations

by Zora Getmansky Hesse

FILTER PRESS
PALMER LAKE, COLORADO
1998

D1398593

FILTER PRESS
WILD AND WOOLLY WEST BOOKS

Post Office Box 95
Palmer Lake, Colorado 80133
(719) 481-2420

Choda	Thirty Pound Rails, 1956
Clemens	Celebrated Jumping Frog, 1963
Cushing	My Adventures in Zuni, 1967
Matthews	Navajo Weavers and Silversmiths, 1968
Campbell	Wet Plates and Dry Gulches, 1970
Banks	Alferd Packer's Wilderness Cookbook, 1969
Faulk	Simple Methods of Mining Gold, 1969, 1981
Rusho	Powell's Canyon Voyage, 1969
Hinckley	Transcontinental Rails, 1969
Seig	Tobacco, Peace Pipes and Indians, 1971
Scanland	Life of Pat F. Garrett, 1971
Arpad	Buffalo Bill's Wild West, 1971
Powell	The Hopi Villages, 1972
Schwatka	Among the Apaches, 1974
Bourke and	General Crook in the Indian Country *and*
Remington	A Scout with the Buffalo Soldiers, 1974
Powell	An Overland Trip to the Grand Canyon, 1974
Harte	Luck of the Roaring Camp, 1975
Remington	On the Apache Reservations *and*
	Among the Cheyennes, 1974
Bryan	Navajo Native Dyes, 1978
Underhill	Pueblo Crafts, 1979
Underhill	Papago & Pima Indians of Arizona, 1979
Bennett	Genuine Navajo Rug, How to Tell, 1979
Kennard	Field Mouse Goes to War, 1977
Underhill	People of the Crimson Evening, 1982
Choda	West on Wood, Volume 1, 1986
Duran	Mexican Recipe Shortcuts, 1983
Roosevelt	Frontier Types in Cowboy Land, 1988
Young	Kokopelli, 1990
Garrod	Coyote and the Fish, 1993
Williams	Cripple Creek Conflagrations, 1993
Duran	Kid Kokopelli, 1995

SOUTHWESTERN INDIAN RECIPE BOOK
Copyright © 1998 Filter Press
ISBN 0-86541-042-9 paper
Printed in the United States of America

Publisher's Note

Long before the coming of whites to the Southwest, Indians had efficient agricultural systems there. Extensive irrigation systems were developed in some locations, supporting such crops as corn, squash, beans, pumpkins, other vegetables, and cotton.

Wild native plants contributed many varieties of fruit, edible flowers, seed, pollen, leaves, bark, and roots. From these were prepared foods as well as dyes, medicines, and materials for weaving and basketry. Cactus fruit and heavy leaves were eaten in most areas. Flowers and fruit of the various squash provided food. Pollen was used as food, but more often was preserved for religious ceremonies. Plant fibers were used for baskets, storage containers, parching trays, garments, and for brushes. Tubes from reeds were used as smoking pipes, and even to make paint sprayers for ceremonial designs. Wood, grass, and manure provided fuel. The Hopi, however, also used coal to fire pottery long before it became an industrial fuel in Europe. These ancient mines are again being developed, and will be the largest coal mines in the world.

Game meat was widely used and was supplemented by domesticated birds, dogs, and a few small animals. The Europeans brought goats, sheep, cattle, and draft animals. These imports added to the variety of meat, as well as the increased productivity of the land by replacing the digging stick with a plow, and permitting carry-ing crops home from more distant productive fields.

The recipes given here are from women of specific tribes. With the exception of local use of a few native plants (saguaro for instance), almost all of these foods were used over a wide range from California to Texas, and from Mexico

Apache fiddler and maiden

to Colorado, Utah, and Nevada. The picture of the Zuni garden (page 44) was equally typical of village gardens in many parts of the Southwest.

Some cultures lived in large permanent villages, with reliable water supplies and productive farmlands. Some moved between summer and winter homes. Some spent part of the season following game and wild plants as they developed. Almost all used pottery, baskets, stone grinders, and woven fabrics. Pottery was often made at temporary camps, to be abandoned when the group returned to their other homes. Artistic patterns were left off the temporary pots, but they served the same functions as those ornately decorated for use in the permanent settlements.

Foods were usually preserved by drying and parching. There is some evidence that freezing was used among the northern pueblos. The fire pit baffles in some kivas could have drawn cold winter air across meats. If these were then wrapped and buried in corn husks, bark, or other insulating materials, they would have remained frozen for several months.

When the whites brought goats, sheep and cattle they were eagerly accepted. Coffee in particular became a favorite trading-post item. At the same time, Indian foods became an important part of the colonists' diets. This interchange contributed to today's wonderful assortment of Southwestern and Mexican foods.

The Pueblos at Zuni, in the Hopi Villages, and along the Rio Grande were more completely described and illustrated in the 19th century than those of other areas. Therefore the pictures of village life included in this booklet are more complete for the villages still seen by tourists in the Southwest. The early explorers and writers seem to have taken the same tours as we do today!

Mrs. Hesse has given us original Indian recipes as well as others which are merely a few hundred years old and include the use of the "new" foods introduced by the Spanish.

Introduction

Corn, squash, beans and pumpkin are integral parts of Southwest Indian ritual and religion. These foods were prominent in ancient legend and have been passed down through the generations from unrecorded time to the present. Their form is found in sacred paintings; special songs are sung as the seeds are planted; and all who have experienced the joyful Corn Dance know the intimacy, harmony, and intangible bond between Mother Earth and her children.

Beneath the sands of centuries-in ancient cave dwellings, and in long-abandoned mesa-top and canyon villages-archeologists have found seeds of these staples stored in baskets and pottery jars by peoples who were ancient when Europe was young.

Almost every recipe in this book includes at least one of these life staples of the Southwest.

The recipes marked with a small basket originated before the first contact with European culture. Those without a basket are acculturated recipes; Indian, to be sure, but with ingredients added through the mingling of peoples of the unique Southwest.

Although wheat flour is now used as a thickener, originally flours were prepared from various seeds and native grains. Wheat was first used in the late 18th Century and its use may certainly be regarded as traditional.

Most of the ingredients used in these recipes are available in supermarkets and grocery stores throughout the Southwest and in specialty shops elsewhere in the country. Canned roasted green chili can be substituted for the fresh variety; for those who prefer milder tasting foods, green bell peppers can be used as a last resort.

Tepary beans can only be bought on the Pima reservation in south-central Arizona. Mesquite beans, cholla buds, squawberries, and prickly pear are nature's desert bounty.

Due to differences of altitude and ovens, cooking times and oven temperatures may have to be adjusted slightly. Although most of the recipes were tested at Albuquerque's 5000 ft. elevation, a number of the Pima recipes were tested at Sacaton, Arizona, practically at sea level.

Many friends—Pima, Pueblo, and Navajo—helped with these recipes and gave me their encouragement. Since they prefer to be nameless, they know they have my silent thanks.

To my family: Frank, David, Debby, and Teva—who ate through countless failures and successes of these recipes—all my love.

Z.G.H., Albuquerque, New Mexico

Table of Recipes

Women grinding corn

Zuñi water jar

Aboriginal
Recipe

Kneel-down Bread
Navajo

INGREDIENTS

5 ears corn with husks

DIRECTIONS

Carefully remove husks from corn, dampen with water and set aside.

Scrape kernels from cob.

Grind corn kernels to a pulp on a metate.

Make a layer of corn husks and place corn pulp on top. Cover with more husks and form into a package. Place this package in hot ashes with some hot coals on top. Cook for 1 hour.

This old-time cornbread is known as "kneel-down bread" because that is the position you assume when grinding on a metate.

For modern cooking: Husk 5 ears of corn. Scrape kernels from cob and mash kernels to a pulp with a wooden pounder. Two well beaten eggs can be added to corn pulp for more cohesiveness. Shape pulp into a loaf and place on aluminum foil; then wrap into a package. Place in 350° oven for 1 hour. Or place under hot ashes with hot coals on top.

Variations: Chopped, seeded and peeled green chili and/or chopped tomatoes can be added to corn pulp.

This is a good dish for camping.

Blue Corn Bread
Navajo

Aboriginal
Recipe

INGREDIENTS

½ cup juniper ashes
½ cup boiling water
3 cups blue cornmeal
1 ¾ cups boiling water

DIRECTIONS

Burn green part of juniper until you get ½ cup of ashes.
Mix into ½ cup boiling water. Strain ashes through colander and set aside.

In pot, bring to a boil 1 ¾ cups water. Add juniper ashes
and stir. Add 3 cups blue cornmeal and stir. Cool.

Knead until a soft, firm dough is formed. Shape into
a loaf and wrap in foil. Place in 350° oven for 1 hour.

Cooking breakfast

Navajo Paper Bread
Navajo

INGREDIENTS

1 cup juniper ashes

1 cup boiling water

1 cup blue cornmeal

3 cups boiling water

DIRECTIONS

Burn the green juniper, not the branch part, until you
get 1 cup of ashes. Mix into 1 cup boiling water. Strain
through colander and set aside.

Bring 3 cups of water to boil in pot. Stir in juniper ashes.
Stir in 1 cup of blue cornmeal. Cool.

Very lightly grease a griddle and heat. When hot, carefully
spread by hand as thin a layer as possible of the cornmeal
batter. Flatten with spatula if necessary. Do not turn.
Remove from griddle as batter is cooked.

Zuñi ladel

Navajo Fry Bread
Navajo

INGREDIENTS

4 cups white flour
1 tablespoon baking powder
1 teaspoon salt

DIRECTIONS

Mix the above ingredients together. Add 1½ cups warm water to dry ingredients. Knead until dough is soft and elastic and does not stick to bowl. (If necessary add a little more warm water.)

Shape dough into balls the size of a small peach. Pat back and forth by hand until dough is about ½ or ¼ inch thick and round. Make a small hole in center of round.

Melt 1 cup lard or shortening in heavy frying pan. Carefully put the rounds into hot fat, one at a time. Brown on both sides. Drain on paper towels and serve hot.

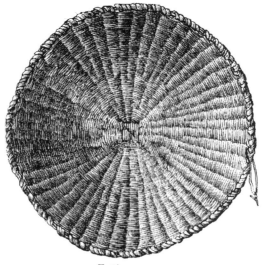

Zuñi mat

An Easier Navajo Fry Bread
Navajo

INGREDIENTS

2 cups white flour
2 teaspoons baking powder
½ cup powdered milk
½ teaspoon salt

DIRECTIONS

Mix the above ingredients together. Add warm water, a little at a time, to form a dough. Knead until dough is soft and not sticky. Cover bowl with cloth and let stand for 1 hour.

Shape into small balls. On a lightly floured surface roll with rolling pin into circles ½ to ¼ inch thick.

Put ½ inch of lard or shortening in heavy skillet. Test for hotness by putting pinch of dough in skillet. If it browns quickly but does not burn, the fat is at the right temperature. Place the circles of dough—one at a time—into the skillet. Brown on both sides and drain on paper towels.

Apache in 19th century dress

Aboriginal
Recipe

Blue Corn Bread
Pueblo

MIX TOGETHER

1½ cups blue cornmeal

2 teaspoons baking powder

3 tablespoons sugar

MIX TOGETHER

¾ cup milk (skim milk can be substituted)

1 egg

3 tablespoons bacon drippings

4 oz. canned, chopped green chili

DIRECTIONS

Put liquid ingredients into dry ingredients and mix well.

Pour into greased baking pan and put in 350° oven for
30 minutes or until wooden toothpick comes out clean.

VARIATIONS

2 tablespoons minced onion

½ cup raisins

½ cup minced bacon

Any combination can be added to the batter
before cooking.

Pueblo Oven Bread
Pueblo

INGREDIENTS

1 package dry yeast

¼ cup warm water

½ tablespoon lard or shortening

¼ cup honey or sugar

1 cup hot water

5 cups all purpose flour

DIRECTIONS

Dissolve yeast in ¼ cup warm water, mix well and set aside.

In large mixing bowl mix lard, honey and salt. Add 1 cup hot water and stir well. When mixture cools to room temperature, combine with yeast mixture and mix well.

Add 4 cups of flour, one at a time, and mix well after each cup.

Spread 1 cup of flour on a chopping board and turn dough mixture onto it. Knead for about 15 minutes until dough is smooth and elastic. Put dough in large bowl, cover with cloth and place in warm area until dough is double in bulk.

Turn dough onto floured surface again and knead well.

Divide dough into two equal parts. Shape the dough into loaves, rounds or into design shape.

Put the two loaves on well-greased cooking sheet, cover with cloth and allow to double in warm area. When doubled, bake in preheated 350° oven for one hour or until lightly browned. Bake the loaves on middle rack of oven. Place a shallow pan of water on bottom rack of oven. This gives the air in the oven the needed moisture for the baking process. In the Pueblos, this bread is baked in outdoor ovens called *hornos.*

San Carlos Apache woman carrying water in a wicker jar

Aboriginal
Recipe

Corn and Pumpkin Stew
Pima, Papago

INGREDIENTS

3 ears corn

1 medium green (unripe) pumpkin

1 cup water

salt to taste

DIRECTIONS

Shell corn from cob and mash into a pulp.

Peel and seed pumpkin and cut into small pieces.

Add water and simmer until pumpkin is soft. Serve hot.

Zuñi water vase

Corn with Squash Blossoms
Pima, Papago

INGREDIENTS

12 squash blossoms

3 ears corn

DIRECTIONS

Boil squash blossoms in small amount of water until tender.

Drain well, mash, and set aside.

Shell corn from cob and boil for ½ hour in water just to cover.

Add mashed squash blossoms and boil gently. Stir frequently until mixture is thick. Season with salt and serve hot.

Walpi meal basket

Prickly Pear Vegetable
Pima, Papago

DIRECTIONS

Take several tender new leaves of the prickly pear cactus.
Carefully remove thorns. Slice and boil in water to cover
until tender. Or, slice fine and fry in small amount of
cooking oil until tender.

Grinding stones in a Hopi house

Dried Green Chili
Pima

DIRECTIONS

Roast fresh green chili according to directions below.

When chili is cool, peel, remove stem and seeds.

Mash chili into a pulp and form into flat pancake shaped cakes.

Dry outdoors in full sun. Turn often and carefully with spatula to get both sides dried. Bring indoors when the sun starts to go down. This takes two days or more, depending on climate.

Store in covered container until ready to use.

When needed: Pour boiling water over dried chili and let stand until chili becomes plump and soft. Eat at once as relish or use as flavoring when cooking vegetables or meat.

How to Roast Green Chilis

DIRECTIONS

Cover oven rack with aluminum foil.

Wash fresh green chili. Prick with fork on both sides. Place chilis on oven rack and place rack in oven in lower broiler position. Broil until chili is blistered on one side, turn chilis over and broil until blisters form on other side.

Remove from oven and cool.

Roasted chili freezes well and can be stored in freezer for one year without losing freshness. Place cooled roasted chilis in plastic bags, getting as much air out of bags as possible, and tie well. When needed, remove from freezer and defrost in bags or under lukewarm water. Then peel, remove seeds and stems, and use.

Tepary Beans
Pima

This is a very ancient bean grown in the Sonoran desert country from aboriginal times to the present. The beans are either white or brown in color and are used interchangeably.

DIRECTIONS

Wash well and soak 2 cups of tepary beans in water to cover for 12 hours or overnight.

Drain. Add fresh water to cover beans 2 inches higher than beans in large, heavy pot. Cover and simmer for 4 hours or until tender. Add more water if necessary. Add salt to taste.

These beans can be eaten plain with a little butter or:
   with red chili sauce
   with chopped roasted green chili
   with any kind of chili and meat that has been
      cooked separately and then added to beans
   refried with chopped bacon, onions, tomatoes.

Zuñi belt

Cholla Bud Vegetable

Pima, Papago

DIRECTIONS

Carefully pick off yellow cholla buds from the cactus.
Use tongs as the thorns are hard and painful to remove
from fingers.

Place in basket or paper sack. Put cholla buds in large pot
and cover with water. Boil for ½ hour. The thorns will fall
off in the cooking.

Drain in colander and wash well with vegetable brush to
remove any remaining thorns.

Return cholla buds to pot, add fresh water to cover and
simmer until cholla buds are tender. Can be eaten as is
with butter and salt to taste.

Variations after thorns are removed:

24 cholla buds
2 bunches fresh spinach or other greens
Boil cholla buds in water to cover for 45 minutes, add
spinach or other greens and cook 5 minutes more. Drain,
add salt to taste.

24 cholla buds, cooked and sliced
1 small onion, chopped
2 roasted green chilis, peeled and seeded and chopped
½ lb. meat, sliced very thin and in strips
2 tablespoons cooking oil
Put oil in deep skillet. When warm, add all ingredients.
Fry until meat is cooked. Salt to taste and serve hot.

Cliff houses, Rio Mancos, Colorado

Pueblo Dried Red Chili Fry
Pueblo

DIRECTIONS

Wash several dried red chilis in warm water. Remove stems and seeds. Dry with paper towels. Break chilis into moderate sized pieces.

Fry gently for a few minutes in small amount of oil.

Yuma Apache and family building a house

Pueblo Chili Fritters
Pueblo

INGREDIENTS

⅓ cup all purpose white flour

⅓ cup water

1 egg, slightly beaten

½ teaspoon baking powder

½ cup roasted green chili, peeled, seeded and chopped

2 tablespoons minced onion

4 inches cooking oil in skillet or pot

DIRECTIONS

Put flour in mixing bowl. Slowly add water and stir constantly to make a thin sauce. Stir in egg and baking powder. Add chili and onion and mix well.

Heat oil in skillet or pot. Drop batter by tablespoonful into hot oil. Fry until lightly brown. Drain on paper towel and serve hot.

A Pima house

Pima Baked Beans
Pima

Beans are a staple of the Pima diet. They are boiled,
refried, mashed and stewed with vegetables and meat.
This is a tasty dish.

INGREDIENTS

2 cups pinto beans
7 cups water
1 cup bacon, diced
1 onion, chopped
¼ cup brown sugar
½ cup corn syrup
½ teaspoon salt

DIRECTIONS

Wash beans and place in large pot with 7 cups water.
Bring to boil and simmer for 4 hours. Drain and set aside.

In skillet slowly fry bacon. Add onions and fry until onions
are lightly sauteed. Add bacon and onions to beans. Stir
in sugar and corn syrup. Add salt. Pour into ungreased
baking pan and bake in 350° oven for 1 hour.

Zuñi pottery

Pima Peelings Fry
Pima

Considering the high nutritional value of vitamins near the skin of vegetables, this should be called "Vitamin Fry."

INGREDIENTS

6 large raw carrots, scrubbed well

6 medium raw potatoes, scrubbed well

2 tablespoons cooking oil or bacon grease

DIRECTIONS

With potato peeler, thickly peel skins off carrots and potatoes. (Use remainder of carrots and potatoes for another dish.)

Put oil in skillet. When warm, add peelings from carrots and potatoes. Fry over medium heat stirring frequently until done. About 15 minutes. Drain on paper towels and salt to taste.

Decorating pottery **19**

Sacaton Relish

Pima

INGREDIENTS

3 strips lean bacon

3 fresh green chilis, seeded and stems removed

3 medium tomatoes, diced

½ medium onion, diced

DIRECTIONS

In skillet, fry bacon slowly, remove bacon and set aside.

Put chili into bacon grease and fry slowly until tender.

Add onion and fry until onion becomes translucent.

Add tomatoes and fry for 3 more minutes. Add salt to taste. Drain on paper towel and serve.

This relish is good served over scrambled eggs, refried beans, rice or mashed potatoes.

Pimas use very hot chilis. For the uninitiated, mild chili or green bell peppers can be substituted.

Zuñi planting

Navajo Corn and Cheese Pudding
Navajo

INGREDIENTS

2 cups corn kernels, scraped from cob
¾ cup milk
1½ cups yellow cornmeal
⅓ cup melted lard or shortening
2 eggs, beaten well
½ teaspoon baking powder
2 roasted green chilis, peeled, seeded and chopped
1 teaspoon sugar
¼ teaspoon salt

DIRECTIONS

In large mixing bowl put in milk and corn.

Add cornmeal and lard and stir.

Add eggs and baking powder and stir.

Add sugar and salt, then mix in chili and cheese.

Pour into ungreased baking pan and bake in 400° oven
for 45 minutes. Serve hot.

Walpi basket

Blue Corn Mush
Pueblo

INGREDIENTS

1 lb. blue cornmeal
¾ teaspoon double acting baking powder

DIRECTIONS

In 10 inch deep skillet, put in water to ¾ depth of skillet. Bring to boil. Add baking powder and stir.

Add blue cornmeal and stir continuously with wooden spoon. Lower heat to medium. Mixture will become very thick and hard to stir, but continue stirring until mixture is thick and smooth.

Empty into bowl, add salt to taste and serve immediately.

Mush can be dipped into: red chili sauce, sweet syrup or hot milk. Baking powder is the modern substitute for roasted shinbones, which originally supplied calcium carbonate. The sodium carbonate of the baking powder helps to keep the color, as well as the original method.

Navajo woman weaving a belt

Ruined Pueblo and Citadel

24

Meat Jerky
Apache, Pueblo, & Navajo

DIRECTIONS

Lean venison, lamb, mutton or beef can be used. Be sure to use only lean meat without any fat.

Slice meat into thin, ¼ inch slices. Salt moderately well on both sides. Hang meat on line in full sun to dry. Turn from side to side frequently. As sun starts to go down, bring meat indoors to hang in a dry place. Return outdoors the next day in full sun. Depending on climate and humidity, meat will dry in a few to several days. Store in dry place in covered container. Jerky can be eaten as is or used in stews.

Apache basket

Navajo Lamb Loaf
Navajo

INGREDIENTS

2 cups cooked lamb, diced
1½ cups drained stewed tomatoes (or canned tomatoes)
1 cup white bread, diced
½ medium onion, chopped
salt and pepper to taste

DIRECTIONS

In food grinder, grind lamb and put into bowl.

Add remaining ingredients and salt and pepper to taste.
Mix well. Form into a loaf and put into lightly greased
baking pan. Bake in 350° oven for 40 minutes.

Firing pottery

Green Chili Stew
Pueblo

INGREDIENTS

2 lbs. pork, or mutton, lamb, or beef cut in small pieces

3 ears corn with kernels scraped from cob

2 stalks celery, without leaves, diced

2 medium potatoes, peeled and diced

2 medium tomatoes, diced

5 roasted green chilis, peeled, seeded and diced

DIRECTIONS

In large pot, put in enough cooking oil to prevent meat from sticking.

Add meat and cook until meat is lightly browned.

Add rest of ingredients. Add water to cover all. Cover pot and simmer for 1 hour or until done.

Pima basket

Dried Corn with Lamb
Pueblo, Navajo

INGREDIENTS

6 oz. dried corn (chicos), soaked in water to cover
3 dried red chilis
2 lbs. mutton or lamb stew meat
salt to taste

DIRECTIONS

Wash, seed and de-vein red chilis. Put in electric blender
with 1 cup water. Blend until mixture becomes a thin
puree. Set aside.

Cook chicos in twice the water to cover and simmer for
1 hour.

Cook lamb in water to cover in separate pot for
45 minutes. Add chili sauce to chicos. Add lamb and
cook for ½ hour more. Add salt to taste.

This illustrates a recipe devised to prepare mutton which
was introduced by the Spanish explorers.

Tesuke water vase

Hamburger Stew
Pueblo

INGREDIENTS

2 lbs. lean ground beef
1 large onion, chopped
5 medium potatoes, peeled and sliced thin
5 roasted green chilis, peeled, seeded and chopped
2 tablespoons cooking oil

DIRECTIONS

Put oil in skillet. When warm add onion and fry until onion becomes soft. Add meat and stir with fork to break up meat. Fry slowly until meat loses red color. Pour off fat.

Add potatoes and chilis. Stir together and add just enough water to prevent sticking to pan. Cover and simmer slowly until potatoes are soft, about ½ hour. Add salt to taste.

Variations:
　chopped tomatoes
　corn kernels
　green peas
can be added individually or together with potatoes.

Drinking vessels

Aboriginal
Recipe

Backbone Stew with Fresh Corn
Navajo & Pueblo

INGREDIENTS

3 cups corn kernels scraped from cob

3 lbs. mutton or lamb backbone cut into small chunks

3 cups water

DIRECTIONS

Add all ingredients together in large pot. Bring to boil and then simmer for 1½ hours until done. Add salt to taste after cooking.

The backbones used by Indians originally came from wild game.

Apache woman with cradleboard

Navajo Liver Sausage
Navajo

INGREDIENTS
2 lbs. liver
2 medium potatoes, peeled and diced
1 medium onion, diced
2 stalks celery, diced
dash of salt and black pepper to taste
sausage casing from butcher shop

DIRECTIONS
In food grinder, grind all the above ingredients, one at a time. Mix all together very well in mixing bowl.

Put into sausage casings the size of small frankfurters and tie ends well with string.

Place in large pot with water to cover. Bring to boil and then simmer slowly for 1½ hours until done.

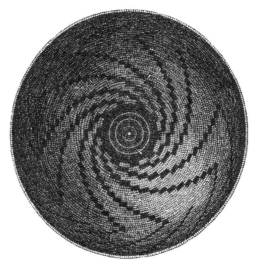

Walpi mat

Mutton or Lamb Stew
Navajo

Any kind of mutton or lamb-cut can be used. For economy this recipe uses neck bones.

INGREDIENTS

2 lbs. mutton or lamb neck bones

6 cups water

3 medium potatoes, peeled and cut into small pieces

1 onion, cut into small pieces

1 stalk celery, without leaves, cut into small pieces

3 roasted green chilis, peeled, seeded and chopped

DIRECTIONS

Put all the ingredients in a heavy pot and bring to a boil. Then simmer for 1½ hours until done. Add salt to taste after cooking is finished.

Carrots, peas, squash, tomatoes and corn can also be used in this stew.

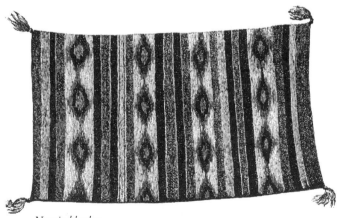

Navajo blanket

Green Pumpkin Stew
Pueblo

INGREDIENTS

1 medium green (unripe) pumpkin, peeled, seeded,
    and sliced

2 ears corn kernels, scraped from cob

1 medium onion, chopped

2 roasted green chilis, peeled, seeded, and chopped

¼ teaspoon garlic powder

2 tablespoons sweet butter or cooking oil

DIRECTIONS

In large pot, melt butter or warm cooking oil. Add pumpkin and onion. Stir frequently and cook slowly until both become translucent.

Add corn, chili and garlic. (The garlic is a recent addition.)

Add just enough water to prevent sticking. Cover and simmer slowly for ½ hour or until done.

Banana or other winter type squash can be substituted for pumpkin.

Wooden bowl

Pueblo Green Jerky Fry
Pueblo

INGREDIENTS

Several slices meat jerky

3 dried green chilis, washed, seeded and diced

½ medium onion, diced

2 tomatoes, diced

1 tablespoon cooking oil

DIRECTIONS

Place jerky in bowl and cover with boiling water until soft. Drain and dry with paper towels. Do the same with dried green chilis.

In frying pan add oil. When warm add onion, jerky, chili. Fry gently until onion starts to brown. Add tomatoes and fry five minutes more.

Stone steps at Oraibi

Aboriginal
Recipe

Red Chili Stew
Pueblo

INGREDIENTS

2 lbs. pork, cut into small pieces (save some fat)
5 dried red chilis
½ teaspoon oregano powder
¼ teaspoon garlic powder
salt to taste

DIRECTIONS

Wash chilis. Remove stems and seeds. Place in electric blender with 1 cup water and blend into a paste. Set aside.

In deep skillet put in pork fat until bottom of skillet has enough fat to prevent meat from sticking. Discard remaining fat.

Add pork to skillet and fry until lightly browned.

Add chili paste and mix well with meat. If too thick, add a little more water. Add oregano and garlic. Cover skillet and simmer slowly for 1 hour until done. If sauce becomes too thin add enough cornstarch to thicken and mix well to prevent lumps.

This recipe can also be used for pork chops or lamb or beef stew meat.

Walpi water vase

19th Century Southwestern Indian Village

Pumpkin and Corn Dessert
Pima

INGREDIENTS

1 small, ripe pumpkin

2 ears corn

½ cup whole wheat flour

sugar or honey to season

DIRECTIONS

Peel, seed, and slice pumpkin. Cover with water and cook until tender.

Shell corn from cob and place kernels on pie tin in 350° oven and bake for 15 minutes.

Add corn to pumpkin. Add flour, stirring continuously until mixture thickens. Do this over low heat. Add sugar or honey to taste. Serve hot.

Zuñi water jar

Aboriginal
Recipe

Mesquite Bean Dessert
Pima, Papago

DIRECTIONS

The measurements are 1 tablespoon whole wheat flour to each 1 cup of mesquite bean juice (see page 42).

Put mesquite bean juice in pot. Bring to boil. Add flour to juice very slowly and stir continuously until mixture thickens. Cool and serve.

Weaving on diamond-shaped diagonals

Squawberry Dessert
Pima, Papago

DIRECTIONS

Pick and wash squawberries. Mash berries and put into pot half filled with water. The seeds will sink to the bottom of the pot. Remove berries with serrated cooking spoon. Discard old water and seeds.

Return mashed berries to pot and cover with water. Boil slowly for 20 minutes. Add whole wheat flour to thicken and stir frequently. Add sugar to taste. Cool and serve.

Navajo blanket

Navajo Blue Cake
Navajo

INGREDIENTS

3 cups water
2 cups blue cornmeal
1 cup yellow cornmeal
1 cup raisins
½ cup sprouted wheat
¼ cup brown sugar

DIRECTIONS

Bring water to boil in large pot. Add all ingredients—
one at a time—to water. Stir well with a wooden spoon
until mixture is smooth. Pour into aluminum foil lined
pan. Cover with more foil.

Bake in 300° oven for 2 hours. Test by putting a wooden
toothpick in middle of cake. If toothpick comes out clean,
the cake is done.

Making Zuñi He-We (Paper Bread)

Wheat Pudding Dessert
Pueblo

INGREDIENTS

2 cups panocha flour (germinated wheat flour)
¼ cup white flour
4 cups boiling water
¾ cup sugar
1 tablespoon fat or sweet butter
½ cup water

DIRECTIONS

Mix wheat and white flour together in mixing bowl.

Pour boiling water into flour mixture. Stir with wooden spoon until smooth. Texture should be like smooth pancake batter.

In small pot put sugar, fat or butter, and ½ cup water. Stir continuously over low heat until mixture comes to a boil.

Pour into flour mixture and stir until well blended.

Turn into lightly greased baking dish and bake uncovered in 350° oven for 1 hour. Let cool but serve warm.

This is a very rich pudding.

Variations:
> ¾ cup raisins can be added to batter but reduce sugar to ⅓ cup.
> Milk, cream or ice cream can be used for topping.

Mesquite Bean Juice Drink
Pima, Papago

Aboriginal
Recipe

DIRECTIONS

Pick the yellow soft beans of the mesquite bush in July.
Clean and place in large pot with water to cover.
Boil until beans are tender. Cool in pot.

With wooden pounder, pound mesquite beans until
pulpy. Drain through colander, saving liquid for the juice.
This is an ancient and refreshing drink.

A camp

Pima Pinole

Pima

INGREDIENTS

½ cup blue cornmeal
2 tablespoons sugar
½ teaspoon cinnamon

DIRECTIONS

In dry frying pan add blue cornmeal, stirring constantly over high heat until corn meal begins to brown. Remove from heat and put into jar. Add sugar and cinnamon and stir well. Cool. Cover jar and store until needed.

A few teaspoons of this mixture can be stirred into milk or water for a nourishing drink. Or, larger amounts can be added to milk or water to form a cereal.

Variation:

Whole wheat flour can be substituted for blue cornmeal and used in the same manner.

In the very early days, honey and native spices were used instead of the sugar and cinnamon.

Hopi tray

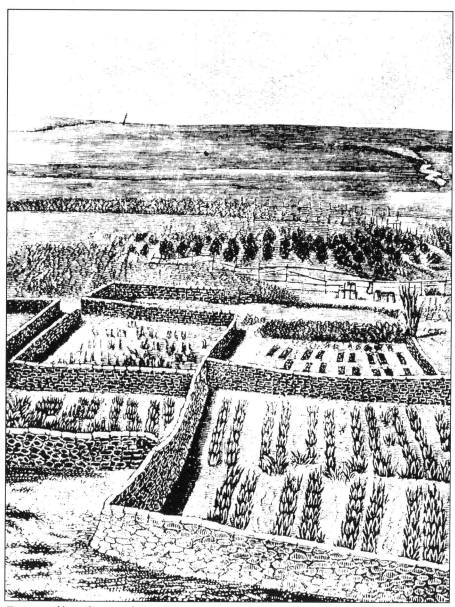

Zuñi vegetable garden in 19th century